A *Special Angel,*
A *Special Friend*

Bernadette Lindemer

PAGE PUBLISHING, INC.
Conneaut Lake, PA

First originally published by Page Publishing 2021

ISBN 978-1-6624-5359-5 (pbk)
ISBN 978-1-6624-5360-1 (digital)

Printed in the United States of America

CHAPTER 1

Don't Be Afraid
I Will Carry You

He died on a sunny Monday morning the second day in December. The night before was stormy and windy. The winds whipped and howled so loudly against his hospital room window. The hollow keening sound of banshees battered my ears, and all I could do was pray.

I wrapped myself tightly in the hospital blanket a nurse gave me. I decided to spend the night in my husband's room with him rather than go home only to be called in the middle of the night to be summoned to his side.

I called his mother early Sunday morning, frantic and tearful, wondering how I was going to break the news to her that her only son, my husband, Jim, was dying.

Jim's yearlong battle with the insidious disease, lung cancer, had finally come to a close. For twelve long months in 1996, Jim and I faced every day with the reality that his time on earth was limited but also with the fantasy that maybe, just maybe, we could be the exception to the rule. Reality won.

The winter months that followed were bleak and lonely. Although there was a steady stream of family, friends, and coworkers offering company and support, it always brought out the crushing realization that I was a widow and I was alone.

About six months before Jim was diagnosed, I had a dream of a tall dark-haired stranger. He is handsome and is dressed in a dark suit and trench coat. We are both waiting at a bus station. He is standing behind me. I have no idea where I am going. Suddenly, he puts his right hand on my right shoulder and turns me toward him. I look into his face. It is familiar to me, but I am not quite certain of his identity, then he lifts me and holds me in his arms, and whispers to me, "Don't be afraid. I will carry you." I wasn't sure what the dream meant, but as I woke from the dream, I vividly remembered the stranger's face. He is my angel, I think, and I believe in his promise.

My nephew, Donald, stayed with me for a couple of weeks to help me get the house organized; we always winterized the deck—putting chairs away, covering things up, cleaning up leaves.

Jim's sports car sat in the garage, a new Miata; he only had it for a few months. He really wanted a Porsche. We previously owned two, and Jim had the fever for exotic cars, and I indulged him. I drove the Miata once or twice. It was leased. I wasn't sure I could keep it, so I returned it to the dealer. They gave me their condolences. I miss that little car; the last memory I have of driving it is the scent of Jim's cologne. Someday, maybe I will get another one, maybe a Porsche. Jim would like that.

The day Jim died, I entered a new dimension, a surrealistic time. I felt myself being sucked into a wormhole. It was as if my mind and body were breaking apart piece by piece. I saw myself going through what I called the dark time. I imagined being spun through a centrifuge, one molecule at a time being drawn into a vortex, and then slowly being put back together, one piece at a time. I remember wanting to be propelled somewhere into the future, wishing it

5

were over. Unfortunately, my dark journey had only just begun.

I tried to occupy my time early into my grieving. I signed up for an art class at the local community college. I was pretty good at oil painting; Jim always encouraged me to paint. I faithfully attended the classes, pushing myself to get to class on time and concentrate on my assignments. I persisted for six weeks, only to withdraw from class because of a lack of commitment.

As the winter dragged on and the snow fell, I began to read self-help books and watched videotapes on grief, loss and dying, and how to cope, hoping I would find an answer that would ease the pain and lessen the loneliness. No answer came. Nothing seemed to help.

I returned to my full-time job in early January, and for eight hours and more a day, my mind was active, and I was busy. I would find myself reaching for the phone to call Jim, only to realize with a cold shudder that he wasn't going to answer the phone anymore. I would never hear his warm, comforting voice again.

As January drew to a close and February's dreary weather arrived, I spent my Sunday mornings in the media room, sitting in front of the big screen TV that Jim bought almost a year before, watching videos of our vacations, hoping to catch a glimpse of him, to hear his voice again, to see him smile at me or call my name. It was like putting butter on a burning wound—it eased the pain for a little while then began to sear again, burning deep into my heart. I missed him.

CHAPTER 2

Memories and Fantasies

I remembered an evening we had spent together, not too long ago, or so it seemed. We watched some videos. We saw the James Bond movie *GoldenEye*. I remembered how we compared the new James Bond, Pierce Brosnan, to the first James Bond, Sean Connery, and agreed that Mr. Brosnan was equally talented and equally handsome. Jim made me laugh.

He said, "Hell, he's so good-looking even I would go out with him."

We laughed and drank wine and watched the movie. I cherished these moments and tried to hang onto each word, glance or touch from Jim, only to be jolted by my mind's cold reality that moments like these were coming to an end.

March was dreary, wet, and cold. Work was consuming me, and for a while, it was okay, but I was always tired, had no motivation, and sometimes even wished that I was somewhere else in the universe. I was depressed. I went to therapy sessions once a week and looked forward to the visits. My therapist was very helpful and offered suggestions for relaxation and meditation. He even gave me some mental exercises that helped me cope with my feelings and relationships, especially toward men. Subconsciously, I was feeling resentful because my husband was dead, and the men I encountered in my personal and business life were still alive. I tensed. Why couldn't it have been the other way around? The exercises helped, and I finally exorcised my demons—my ability to relate to people, men especially, became more relaxed, and I was again able to socialize without feeling resentful.

More snow fell. I had no desire to shovel it. I didn't care if it sealed me inside—at least I would be safe in my own big tomb. My home had become my mausoleum. I listened to our favorite music and tried to lose myself in dreams. I imagined Jim was still with me.

My mother called, every day, to check on her grieving daughter as I once did so long ago after my father died suddenly from a heart attack. I heard my own words echoing in my ears, "Are you eating? Are you getting enough sleep? Has anyone called to ask you to go out?"

Then my mother blurted out, "Oh, I wish you could meet Pierce Brosnan."

I remember wondering to myself what brought that on. Then she told me that "he lost his wife like you lost Jim, you know. I was just standing at the kitchen sink preparing dinner and he just came into my mind, and I thought wouldn't it be something if you could meet him. He's such a nice man." I thought I was hearing things and said that I didn't think someone as famous as Pierce Brosnan would be interested in someone like me.

"Why not?" my mother asked. "You're pretty and still young enough." I told her she was prejudiced. "After all, it's nice to daydream, isn't it?" she asked.

I told her she was right. What's wrong with a little fantasy? It's harmless. That night, I dreamed of Pierce Brosnan. Perhaps he is my bus stop angel.

My mind did a flashback to the summertime and a visit to the hair salon. As I sat down in the chair, a magazine article stared up at me. It was an article on Pierce Brosnan, an interview about his own personal tragedy, the loss of his wife, Cassie Harris, a few years before, to cervical cancer. It was as though someone had purposefully set it there, open to that particular page. I picked it up and began to read. I started to cry and choked back tears, hoping no one would notice. I remember thinking of Jim and me and silently asking God to please spare us. Please, please a miracle for my husband, a miracle for Jim. Please, God, don't send us down that path please God let this cup pass. I choked back more tears and closed the magazine.

I also remembered a customer, sitting in a chair next to mine. He was getting his haircut. He was a chemist, and he was talking about a new cancer drug that was supposed to stop the growth of new cancer cells. His company was awaiting FDA approval before they could proceed with marketing the product. I wanted to reach over and ask him the name of the drug but was too embarrassed. I didn't want him to think I was eavesdropping.

Moreover, I didn't want to expose my husband. We both frequented the same salon. Jim was a very private person. He didn't want to talk about his illness. He said he didn't want pity. Only close family members and some close friends knew about Jim. I respected Jim's desire for privacy, but I was sorry I didn't ask about the cancer drug.

CHAPTER 3

Singapore

April just showed up one morning. The tulips near our front door burned bright red in the sunlight. The trees surrounding our home began to bud. I watched as if through Jim's eyes as the backyard view, Jim loved so much, became a panorama, first of buds of light green and deep red and then beautiful deep green leaves. I remembered one summer afternoon, a few years before, the trees began to spread out and mature. Jim bet me that he could predict when the silver maples planted closest to the deck would touch. I lost.

Jim loved trees, and every chance we got, we planted trees—all kinds of trees. It didn't make a difference. Every year that we spent Christmas at home, we bought a live tree, and every year, we planted it. I nicknamed Jim Johnny Appleseed, an avid apple tree planter and defender of the environment, and I happily supported his endeavor. We were good for each other.

April wore on with no end in sight. We loved the spring and summer months. Jim and I shared an affinity for the warm weather. We looked forward to our weekends with planting and gardening and just enjoying the warm sunny days. I remember those spring mornings when the earth came alive with such radiant colors, birds singing and nesting in our trees, the sun shining warmly on the misted grass, and Jim's observation, "It's a beautiful day in the neighborhood," would always make me feel happy, safe, comfortable, and most importantly, glad to be alive. What more could you ask for from life? Our life together was good. Life was sweet, and my husband was alive, and he loved me.

I dreaded my weekends now and had no desire to get out of bed. I used to look forward to Saturday mornings. The coffee aroma would fill the house. Jim would turn on the TV—one of his favorite shows was the *Muppets*. Jake and Tess, our dogs, would pad around the house, following him, barking their requests for breakfast. The house would come alive with the sounds of Jim.

The only sounds I heard now were the eerie sounds of silence. Getting up became a chore, I preferred the darkness of my bedroom to the warm spring sunlight. Damn this loneliness, damn death.

April dragged its feet. Close personal friends of ours, Karen and Wayne, invited me to vacation with them in Singapore in May. I accepted. I joked around with Karen—maybe this would be an opportunity for me to meet someone intriguing "James Bond" perhaps. I told her about my Pierce Brosnan fantasy. She humored me and indulged my fantasy. The trip was wonderful; Singapore is one of the most beautifully exotic lands in the world. Ten luxurious days in hot, sunny Singapore.

While we were there, we planned a side trip to either Bali or Bangkok. We wanted to end the trip with some simple relaxation and thought either place would be an ideal choice. Karen and I waited too long to make the necessary travel arrangements, so we decided to stay in Singapore and take day trips.

Thursday morning's newspaper arrived in my room. I read it during breakfast. I opened the paper and flipped through the pages. The article read "Pierce Brosnan arrives in Bangkok to begin filming his second James Bond movie." James Bond was next door. I laughed, amused at my own clairvoyance. I told Karen. She was speechless. She said I was psychic.

CHAPTER 4

Needing to Let Go

The end of May approached. I put my house on the market. The house got too big for me. Without Jim, it was nothing, no material possessions, no matter how priceless, could fill the void of losing him. We built this house together. Thirteen years of love and caring went into making our home comfortable, welcoming, and a safe haven for us at the end of our hectic days. Suddenly, the feeling of comfort and safety disappeared; the man who helped to make it so was gone.

June came and went with no prospects of selling my home. I dreaded July's arrival; Jim and I celebrated our respective birthdays in that month. His was the sixteenth, mine the seventh. I remembered his fiftieth birthday surprise party; he thanked me and said he didn't think he would be able to return the surprise. I told him that the only birthday gift I wanted was to have him with me in 1997 and that we would celebrate my birthday with the most expensive bottle of champagne we could find.

My friends invited me over for a Fourth of July party; they surprised me with a cake and gifts. I hope Jim was watching.

I sold the house within two months and had to vacate by the end of August. I needed to find a new home.

The arrival of August and the thought of house hunting brought out very mixed emotions in me. The excitement of a new "premises" and furnishing it piqued my interest but was overtaken by pangs of guilt. I felt I was betraying my husband, deserting our home, our memories. Jim and I were married in August; we celebrated our seventeenth wedding anniversary on August 4, 1996. A mutual friend introduced us in the fall of 1976.

We lived together for three years before we married. We were one year apart in age; I thought that was a good thing. We were both successful business-people. We had no children, a miscarriage, early in our marriage, brought on massive complications and major surgery. We were told we could try to have children again. No children came. We filled this void by traveling the world and usually planned our trips for the end of August or midfall.

This August was different; the only trip I was planning was to the realtor's to look for a house. I found a premises, a jumping-off point. The house was comfortable, and all my furniture fit into it very well. I packed up and moved into my new home on August 22, 1997. Memories, fortunately, are portable. I took them with me, and I didn't look back.

I know that someday I will find the real premises, and when I do, I will make my home there. I am visited again by a dream of Pierce Brosnan. He is in a sports car, sitting next to me. He is casually dressed in jeans, a turtleneck, and a leather jacket. The smell of leather fills my senses. A teenage boy is with him. He speaks to me and asks me if I want to go for a ride. I accept. He kisses me on the cheek. The dream ends. As I relive the dream, I interpret it as dream transference. Mr. Brosnan represents my husband. Jim and the young teenager represent the child we never had. It was a good dream. I feel better.

September was a busy month. I traveled a lot. Some for fun, some for business.

I visited my sister in Dallas. I hadn't been to visit Debbie and Mike for over eighteen years. They took me to Downtown Dallas. We ate delicious food and listened to some great jazz. We felt young again. We had fun.

Friends of mine invited me to join them for Irish Weekend at the Wildwood Shore. We stayed at a local motel. Four women cramped in a one-room motel room with a bath. We drank beer, sang songs, reminisced about our lives, and danced to some great music. We went to a concert. The group Blackthorne played. I had never heard them before. I never danced so much in my life. I think I managed to lose five pounds. I would like to do it again next year.

CHAPTER 5

Moving through the Wormhole

October was looming, and I did all that I could to put the events of 1996 away in my mental storage chest. I wanted to avoid venturing into my dark time as much as possible. I thought that I was finally coming through the wormhole. Unfortunately, the worst days lay ahead, and I did not want to think about them.

October arrived. I am haunted by memories of the year before. I try not to go back to them. I feel that if I do, I am not giving Jim the ability to cross-over in peace and that I am in some way holding back his soul from the journey he must take. I dream about him; the dreams are so real, and he is whole and well again and so beautiful to see. I am encouraged by these dreams, and for a while, I am uplifted.

Toward the end of October, I visited my sister Joyce and her husband, John, in North Carolina. They had been trying to convince me, for some time, that I should move to North Carolina. They even took me house hunting one day and pointed out a house that they humorously called Bernie's House. It was in their neighborhood and had been up for sale. I decided to take a look at it and discovered that it was just what I was looking for. I found the premises, the house of my dreams, and I bought it.

Another dream visits. This time, I dream of Mr. Brosnan once again. He is kind and friendly and invites me to his home for dinner. It is a nice dream. We talk. It's a friendly visit. The dream ends. I feel better. There is comfort in these dreams. I interpret this to be the sign of a kindred spirit. We both experienced a similar personal tragedy, which can only be understood by those who have traveled this road. Without truly realizing it myself and unbeknownst to him, Mr. Brosnan is helping me through my dark times, through the wormhole.

I am afraid to face November but cannot avoid it. The sinister hooded specter that haunted us last year was again looming at the door. I let him in.

Thanksgiving approached, and I choked. I did not want to be alive; memories of the last

Thanksgiving came flooding back. Jim was undergoing aggressive treatment for his cancer. He seemed to be holding his own. He worked full-time up to that Tuesday before Thanksgiving. We tried as best we could to live a normal lifestyle. Jim was an enigma; he was so beautifully strong. By Thanksgiving Day, however, the aggressive treatment caught up with him. He was too weak to attend Thanksgiving dinner and insisted that I go alone to my mother's. I stayed just long enough to eat and then hurried back home to Jim. I took him some dinner and dessert. He ate it, but he was so tired he could hardly hold the fork in his hands. He said the dessert was best. It felt so soothing in his throat. By Friday, Jim could hardly get his socks on. I took him to the hospital he never came out. Three days later, Jim was gone.

My family is coming for Thanksgiving this year. My sister and her husband and my brother and his wife are coming to be with my mother this year. I offer my home to them since I will be away for the holiday. I decided to visit my mother-in-law in Alabama. I made the travel arrangements—a difficult decision since Jim and I spent quite a few Thanksgivings with his mom and dad. I am apprehensive about this visit but know I must go and face this fear alone.

In preparation for my family's arrival, I go to the market. Since they were also babysitting my puppies, I wanted to make sure they had enough food to eat. I move swiftly through the aisles, fruit, vegetables, meat, milk, and ice cream. I want to get this shopping over with; I remember with reluctance the shopping I did for Thanksgiving past when Jim and I hosted the Thanksgiving meal. I don't want to cry. I push the cart faster as I approach the ice-cream freezer. My eye is caught by the magazine stand, located in a most unlikely place, near the ice-cream freezer. Suddenly, my eyes fix on a familiar face staring at me, from the cover of a magazine, it is Pierce Brosnan. The cover story reads: "A new life for the sexy Bond star." I bought it. My shopping chore suddenly got a little easier. My pace slowed, and my heart got a little lighter. Thanks again, Mr. Brosnan, you pulled me through another phase.

My limo arrived at 5:00 a.m. My flight to Alabama was at 7:00 a.m. on Thanksgiving morning. I am facing another dark time. As the limo proceeds to the airport, my mind transports me back to the Thanksgiving trips Jim and I took so many times to see his mom and dad. His dad is dead now, and it is going to be just Mom and me. God, please help me get through this without too much sadness. I arrive at the airport with some time to spare and stop to get a magazine. As I am browsing, there again, right before my eyes is yet another magazine with a cover of Pierce Brosnan. This time, the headlines read: "Pierce Brosnan, the heartbreaking years after his wife's death, the night he finally fell in love again, and the surprising way he and Keely are raising their baby." I bought it and read it on the flight. It helped to put everything into perspective for me and seemed to bolster me with new courage to face the coming holiday with a positive outlook.

Mom and I had a wonderful visit. I came home feeling that, somehow, everything was going to be all right. Thanks again, Mr. Brosnan, you carried me through once again. Perhaps you really are the bus stop angel in my dream.

CHAPTER 6

Discovering Anam Cara

As I said at the beginning of this story, Jim died on December 2, 1996. I remember waking up beside his bed. He had a quiet night, except for the howling winds and rainy weather. I held my rosary in my hands and prayed, asking God to spare him, a miracle for Jim, a miracle for Jim. But by 8:02 a.m. as the sun rose in the sky, Jim's spirit passed over into eternity.

This December 2 loomed over me, and I didn't know whether I wanted to be alone or to be surrounded by people. I left Alabama the Saturday immediately after Thanksgiving, which gave me time to visit with my sister Joyce and her husband, John, before they left for their home in North Carolina. I enjoyed their visit and dreaded their leaving.

I decided to stay home from work that day and spent a quiet, contemplative morning by myself. By noon, I became restless and decided it was better to go to work and be busy than to sit around moping and feeling sorry for myself. One whole year had passed since Jim's death, and finally, I found myself propelled into the future. I was coming through the wormhole, one piece at a time.

December wore on, and Christmas was not too far off. I kept myself busy buying gifts and mailing cards. I received several dinner invitations and even debated on going to North Carolina for the holiday; after all, I would be moving there soon, and perhaps I could take a look at my new home again. I decided, however, that it was best to be still this holiday. I sold my current home during this time and decided to begin the preparations for moving to North Carolina.

As Christmas approached, I decided that I really wanted to be at home for this holiday. I owed it to myself. I hadn't stopped running since Jim died, and now it was time to reconcile with myself, to be still, and finally come to terms with my widowhood.

In between Thanksgiving and Christmas, the new James Bond movie, *Tomorrow Never Dies*, was released. By this time, my whole family was involved in my Pierce Brosnan fantasy, so I was given current, almost daily, updates of Pierce Brosnan sightings. My brother Jim even humored me on a visit one time, searching the internet for Pierce Brosnan news. My sister Joyce even made a special call to me from North Carolina one afternoon to inform me that he was going to be interviewed on Jay Leno that evening and that I shouldn't miss it.

By Christmas Eve, there were so many shows and advertisements for Pierce Brosnan and his new movie that I almost felt like we knew each other. I decided to spend Christmas Eve by myself. I felt that it was an important event in my life that I needed to face on my own.

Jim was a Christmas kind of guy. He loved the holidays with all the celebrations, and almost every year, we hosted a tree trimming party in our home. Jim was known as the consummate host, and although he wasn't very religious, he was always relegated the responsibility for placing the angel on the top of our tree. Last year, at this time I took Jim home to be buried, I was still too numb from the shock of his death to worry about being alone. This year, however, was very different, and I needed this time for my own personal catharsis.

I did a little holiday shopping the weekend before Christmas and decided to visit the local Barnes

& Noble bookstore. While wandering through the aisles of books looking for the appropriate gifts for my staff, I came across a section of specialty books, displayed for the holiday. As I passed by the "special calendars" section, I happened to see a book that intrigued me; the title was *Anam Cara a Book of Celtic Wisdom* by John O'Donohue. Of course, being half-Irish (my other half is Italian), I picked it up and began to read the cover. I was immediately taken in by the description and bought it as a gift for myself.

The Monday before Christmas, I took the day off. I had to undergo a series of medical tests and decided it was best to spend the rest of the day at home. While at home that afternoon, I happened to turn on the TV and saw an advertisement for a program about the making of *007*, the new James Bond movie. It was scheduled to air on Christmas Eve.

Tuesday, I played Mrs. Santa Claus and delivered all the Christmas gifts to my staff and coworkers.

Wednesday, Christmas Eve, I received several invitations to spend this evening with family and friends but decided not to; after all, Pierce Brosnan was going to be around and I didn't want to miss his visit. That evening, I made a special dinner for myself and opened a bottle of champagne and settled in for an evening with Pierce Brosnan.

CHAPTER 7

Finally, through the Wormhole and onto a New Beginning

Christmas morning arrived uneventfully. There were no visitations from any Christmas spirits during the night, and I arose and made myself breakfast and decided to just take it easy. So I began to read my new book *Anam Cara a Book of Celtic Wisdom*. As I read it, I discovered that the title of the book is Gaelic for the words "Soul Friend," and in the prologue, the author reveals that the Anam Cara is a person to whom you could reveal the hidden intimacies of your life and that when you had an Anam Cara, your friendship cut across all convention and category. You were joined in an ancient and eternal way with the friend of your soul.

A SPECIAL ANGEL, A SPECIAL FRIEND

In the first chapter of the book, Mr. O'Donohue describes the mystery of friendship and the fact that the Anam Cara experience opens a friendship that is not wounded or limited by separation or distance. Such friendship can remain alive even when friends live far away from each other. Because they have broken through the barriers of persona and egoism to the soul level, the unity of their souls is not easily severed. When the soul is awakened, physical space is transfigured. Even across the distance, friends can stay attuned to each other and continue to sense the flow of each other's lives. With your Anam Cara, you awaken the eternal. In this soulspace, there is no distance. And we can have more than one Anam Cara in our lifetime, and you don't have to know each other to realize this gift.

I believe that through the similarities of each of our life experiences, Mr. Brosnan has become in spirit an Anam Cara to me without the need to physically meet. The author states that "we do not need to go out to find love, rather we need to be still and let love discover us." I couldn't put the book down; I finished it in less than a day. It is an inspirational work of poetry and words of wisdom. When I finished reading the book, I was compelled to finish this story. I did not want to let this opportunity pass, only to be placed on the shelf of incomplete, well-intentioned, inspired writings, never to be read or heard, as I have done so many times before.

I wanted to take this opportunity first to let the reader know that my husband, Jim, walked this way, even if it was for a short period, and to thank him for being my first Anam Cara, my inspiration, lover, best friend, and mentor. But to also say thank you to my newfound Anam Cara, who has so innocently and unwittingly helped me to overcome my fears of living, loving, and facing my future alone. You have given me fresh hope to do the things I want to do, including opening a scholarship fund, in my late husband's memory with Drexel University, the scholarship is for minorities and women in the areas of civil engineering and computer science. And to thank you, Mr. Brosnan, for helping me to be able to take on, with a lighter heart, the challenges that lie ahead of me.

I now have the premises, the home of my dreams, to which I am moving in early February 1998 and am looking forward to enjoying some incredibly happy times there. As for the Porsche, someday, maybe I will get one again. I love the excitement of sports cars, a bug I caught from Jim. And as for a Pierce Brosnan in my life, well, maybe I will find him and maybe I won't, but whatever the fates hold in store for me, I hope that my Anam Cara will be watching.

The End of the Beginning

ABOUT THE AUTHOR

Bernadette Lindemer (n. Beech) was born in Philadelphia, Pennsylvania, to an Irish-Italian working-class family. She was raised by her father, a police officer, and mother, a housewife, along with her two sisters and one brother.

Bernadette met Jim in 1976, and they married in 1979. Both were professional career people and world travelers. The couple lived happily in Bucks County, Pennsylvania, with their two dogs Jake and

Tess. In 1995, before Jim was diagnosed with lung cancer, Bernadette had a dream of a handsome stranger waiting at a bus stop with her who gave her an unusually cryptic message. After Jim died in 1996, she began to have these strange experiences that were unexplainable. Not wanting to sound crazy to her family and friends, she started to talk about some of her experiences with them and decided to write them down.

She enjoys the arts of writing, oil painting, and music and studied these while attending evening classes at the local community college in Bucks County.

Bernadette currently resides in North Carolina, where she has made her home surrounded by family and friends. She lives with her three rescue dogs, Abby, Gibbs, and Dudley. She still works and continues to write about her spiritual experiences.